*like an angel
dead in your arms*

*like an angel
dead in your arms*

early poems 1995–1999

luke kurtis

like an angel dead in your arms:
early poems 1995–1999

The publication of this book marks the twentieth anniversary of its original edition. This expanded version is the first bd-studios.com edition.

Published by bd-studios.com in New York City, 2020
Copyright © 2000, 2020 by luke kurtis

Design and photography by luke kurtis

ISBN 978-1-950231-95-9

All Rights Reserved. No part of this publication may be reproduced, stored in a retrieval system or transmitted in any form or by any means without the prior permission in writing of copyright holders and of the publisher.

contents

like an angel dead in your arms

i. deviations

carve your own path	14
no eye has seen	15
portrait of a burning daisy	16
congregational oratory	18
defeated victory	21
a dirge	22
let me be	24
i seek You even from the desert	26
the Artist and the box	27
lasciviousness	28
excuse me…	30
wounded	31
a revelation	32

ii. serenades

to mother and father, with love	35
home	36
ode to my own understanding	39
high altitude relief map	40
true love	42
to be	43
goodnight	45
to touch you is like heaven	46
completely free	48
good morning dear heaven	50
in love with you	52
together we become one	54
not long enough	56
animal crackers	58
bedroom	60

iii. requiems

shattered	62
broken up low down dirty heart	64
dead skin cells	66
a lament	68
cayendo	71
your antique angel	72
parting is such sweet sorrow	76
distance	78
lucifer	79
strident utterances of the night	80
woe is my heart	81
a commendation	82
alone, without you	84

other early poems

i. associations

opera	87
mathematics	88
you never know a child	90
existence	92
you ever loved me	95
set my mind up higher	96
stone cast aside	98
where do you stand?	99
shadowed	100
a battle cry	102
purgatory	104
thorn	106
crisp leaves	108

ii. absolutions

a daisy, a fire	111
titanic	112
dark rain	113
come celebrate with me	114
wide-eyed amazement	115
love and art	116
love like a vampire	118
invincible flower	122
absolution	124
faith	125

iii. dimensions

whore	127
my house, my love	128
trapped within you	129
denied your love	130
rosebud	132
reality depth	133
late night past-Times	134
orgasm	137
river run dry	138
for you to find me	140
distant land	142
in dreams i shall forget	143
i miss you bittersweetly	144
rain cloud	145
missing	146
empty	148
i'll find you in the rainbows	150

iv. conclusions

flight	152
i am not here	153
live me well (i'll give you that)	154
burden as i sing	156
convergence	159
an elegy	160
the adage of old age	162
mountaintop discourse	164
i rest within the shadows	165
burning daisies	166
a chant	168

about the artist	170

**like an angel
dead in your arms**

i. deviations

carve your own path (1997)

o little one, small and meek.
your body does not tire so easy.
your body does not grow weak.
and soon you will set out to conquer this place.

as you grow in size and in mind
you begin to ponder the things of this world.
but this world is cruel and unkind.
do not follow its ways. carve your own path.

no eye has seen (1997)

today, somewhere in the world,
a small boy set out on his own,
confident, loving, trusting, caring, believing in himself,
traveling down his road in life.
he knew exactly where it led.

but an evil man, with darkness in his heart,
invaded this boy, and shattered his meaning.
(shattered his complete existenceinto complete nothingness)

the man's eyes saw what they should not see.
the man's hands touched what they should not touch.
the man's mouth tasted what it should not taste.
the man's tongue caressed what it should not caress.

tomorrow, somewhere in the world,
a small boy will hide ever from himself,
terrified, hateful, sad, frightened, afraid of people,
traveling down his road in life
not knowing where it leads.

portrait of a burning daisy (1999)

flowers growing
atop mountains
ignite flames that reach
toward heaven.

but my soul reaches for heaven
and it is out of range.
i am unable to grasp it.

marigolds and roses grow
from sunrays in the sky,
while moonflowers grow
under the night
and never see any daylight.

i am a moonflower
who stands alone.
my existence has become
beautiful yet horrifying.
like a bonfire

i burn vigil in the night,
but sunlight overwhelms,
dousing my daytime stardom.

sometimes i feel
this overwhelming urge
to inflict pain upon myself
to confirm the fact that
i need defeat more than anything,
even more than love.

dying is my essence of living,
another term for death.
how would you react?

congregational oratory (1997)

    alone
    in a place where there are supposed
        to be others
    who understand,
    care and love.
    in a place where your needs
        (both good and bad)
    are supposed to be filled.

    they have left me
        to brutally starve
    and suffer unnecessary pain
    day after day,
        hour after hour.
            sometimes even minute after minute.
                or perhaps, second after second.

but the measure is not important,
just the fact itself.
time has no meaning
    under the sun.
just a mere distraction
    from what is really important,
and what our eyes should be focused on.

defeated victory (1997)

trapped inside my world, this ball of fire,
consumed by burning daisies, i'm nothing but a liar.
can't you just let me be and leave my soul alone?
can't you somehow mend these shattered, broken bones?

i search for an empty place to fill with my void.
i search for a lonely place to love and call my own.
will i find a place to stay and have security
or will i remain alone in this vast expanse of solitude?

i block the path that leads to my history
and try to fight conceit.

will i lose this battle with victory
or win it with sincere defeat?

a dirge (1999)

my inner voice breaks
as i rest on the ground,
unable to move
at my sheer astonishment.

my eyes hide a secret
unknown to daylight
and like a wilted daisy
i stand in a droop.

the war for uniformity
battles against my soul,
waging missile warfare
to find my treasure.

born a beauty
the earth scorched me,
pivoted me to hate,
tearing at me.

unleashing brutal carnage
and bloody flesh,
ahead into the fire
i am thrusted.

my raveled body reeks,
my hair smells of sulfur.
i descend into the ashes,
burying myself alive.

let me be (1996)

i lead a life with eyes so blind
free your soul, release your mind
in this hell i can't survive
wasted love and wasted time

down in the depths of this place
my fears alone i cannot face
i look for my past, but it's erased
i live my life in walls encased

i see in the darkness
freeze in your warmness
find comfort in my pain
let me be, let it rain

it's all a dark and dreadful dream
lost forever is how it seems
i walk to the edge, i look as i lean
let me be, just let me be

i see in the darkness
freeze in your warmness
find comfort in my pain
let me be, let it rain

left alone in solitude
i find myself and then i lose
then i see i'm saved from sin
as i fall into Your hand

setting sun and salty tears
a new love saves me from my fears
as i learn to love, adore
i leave myself behind once more

i see in the darkness
freeze in your warmness
find comfort in my pain
let me be, let it rain

i seek You even from the desert (1997)

when i am lost in the desert and my soul is thirsty
    and tired
You bring water to my lips and save me from the Fire

when i see Your presence in this place i behold Your
    glory and Your power
my lips will offer up Your praise until my final hour

when i think of You through the watches of the night
i sing in the shadows of Your wings, You make my
    wrongs all right

when they seek my life they will be given over to Your
    sword
they will be destroyed, You will protect me Lord

protect me dear Spirit, and keep me from harm
save me somehow, save me dear God

the Artist and the box (1997)

once i heard someone say
"God is a concept by which we measure our pain."
but i never believed that.

refusing all ironies beyond my comprehension.
pretending i alone know the truth.
placing my beliefs behind barricaded doors.

but somehow i realized my faith can be unrestricted
and i don't have to place limits on the details.

you cannot place all creation inside a box.
the vast expanse of existence is beyond boundary.
therefore, you cannot place the Creator in a box either.
for isn't creation just an extension of the Creator?

lasciviousness (1997)

your beauty,
    your body,
        your love,
            your sex.
i covet it all,
    each and every last part.
but especially your sex.

my lust overtakes me.
i feel my raging stature
    reach towards the sky
        in my own erection.
i feel my raging fluid
    reach towards the sky
        inside my own erection.

i fear the day
    i act upon my lust.
will that day ever arrive?
will the calendar prove its existence?

or will i always bring
    this pleasure to myself
        with my hand
            in the dark
                of the night?

excuse me... (1997)

excuse me father, i'm not what you want me to be
i pray that you'll forgive me, i'm down on bended knee
i've grown to love what you hate, it's a part of me
i'm sorry we can't be the same, i'm speaking honestly

excuse me mother, i'm not what you want me to be
i pray that you'll forgive me, i'm down on bended knee
i've learned to love what you hate, it's a part of me
i'm sorry we can't be the same, it's not my choice you see

excuse me sister, i'm not what you want me to be
i pray that you'll forgive me, i'm down on bended knee
i've learned to love what you hate, it's a part of me
i'm sorry we can't be the same, it's just my honesty

wounded (1997)

i pour myself out to you,
but you pull me down and rip at my flesh
like a vulture upon its prey.
your cold-blooded destruction of me
brings chill bumps to my arms,
and even the more sensitive areas of my body.

you rip and pull at the open flesh wounds
up and down my arms,
my back, my legs.
you pour salt upon my bloodstained cuts,
and spit into the open cavities upon my appendages.

i came from your body,
but yet you destruct my body.
i once loved you,
but you have caused me to hate you
more than life itself.

a revelation (1999)

sometimes i feel i'm nothing
but a burning daisy
in a world of frozen roses.

fiery passion
surrounded by ice,
petals never melting
for they are frozen
in conformity.

an alien in this land,
this world's not my home.
i seek something greater.

douse the flames
and spread my ashes,
so that i may
know what it's like
to be a frozen rose.

i learn the way of roses
and understand that which
i can never be.

but after a time,
gather my ashes
and set me on fire,
for i will always be
a burning daisy.

ii. serenades

to mother and father, with love (1998)

it's a blood-stained reality
what all you used to do to me.
and i haven't spent my time trying to forget,
only trying to rearrange.

how can you even live with yourself
when all you've done is cause such hell?
maybe you don't feel at all,
so you don't know what hurting's like.

a cold bitter night seems to do the trick
and lays men down and makes them sick.
do you ever think about what i feel?
i fear not, for my words mean nothing to you.

i've moved away from you now. i'm free,
though it's hard to forget your insanity.
but know i love you as much as ever
and in my heart your memory remains.

home (1998)

lately the bathroom is my favorite place to be.
i'm not sure why. maybe the sound of silence,
or a sense of privacy.
but it's where i feel at home.

i've never understood our need for home.
i guess it secures life somehow,
gives us something of our own.
it's something you can't take away.

then why do we run away?
i guess it makes the most sense sometimes
to find another place to stay.
but it only makes sense if you're hurting.

i think home is a state of mind
where we can see the dark shadows of our past,
or if we want, leave them behind.
whatever we do, at home it's our choice.

ode to my own understanding (1998)

out on your own again,
fighting the direction of the wind.
but were you listening to
the music this time around?

completely unknown you go
against the grain of the world.
but why go with the grain?
it's much too rough for my feet.

roll against the tide
and seek what truth you find.
back home you're just a memory
of all the things you used to be.

to them you've burned out,
cold in the black night.
but really you're just fading away
into what you will become.

high altitude relief map   (1998)

there's something inside us all.
it's just a matter of
mapping out the territory
before we find out what it is.

before any diamond is mined
or gold is panned,
you have to hold
a map to that place.

don't walk away from yourself,
and don't turn your back on humanity.
together we hold the answer.
love is gentle and sincere my friend.

when i call your name,
stop and take a deeper look
at what's inside of me.
know me for what i am.

you can depend on me.
and i will be there in the end.
together we will see
what it means to be a friend.

true love (1998)

do you think true love ever really exists,
or is it one of those old-fashioned myths?

do you think true love ever really stays,
or does it wake up the next morning only to go away?

do you think true love ever really lasts,
or does it wind up as a fading memory passed?

do you think true love is ever really true?
if so, i only want it with you.

to be (1998)

to be in love
to be given life
to be given a home

to be given trust
to be given hope
to be given memories

to be given joy
to be given peace
to be given happiness

to be given warmth
to be given touch
to be given taste

to be given love
to be given you
to be given love with you

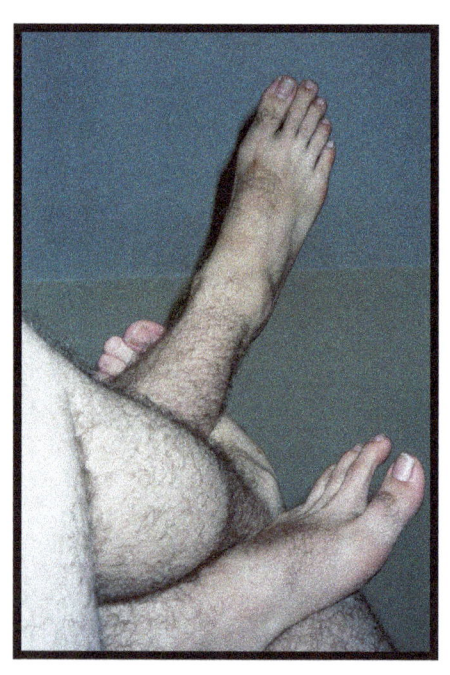

goodnight (1998)

my love, my love do you know
the rain falls sweet and kind of slow?
do you know how i feel
and that my love for you is real?
do you know that dreams are true
and all my dreams i dream of you?
i say goodnight as you drift away,
i will see you tomorrow, another day.

to touch you is like heaven (1998)

with all the world against my back
and nothing but a prayer in hand,
i walk away in hopes of seeing you.

it's so hard to feel pretty these days
and as i get older, memories fade.
i need you to keep me going.

without you my life would be empty
and i could never sleep at night again,
for you wouldn't be there to warm me.

and there's nothing i cherish more
than feeling your breath against my back
while listening to sounds your body makes.

to touch you is like heaven.

completely free (1997)

i never knew what it meant to be
completely free
i never knew what it meant to say
you'd love someone just to have your way
there's a world of things i never knew,
but that didn't stop me from loving you

you have comforted me more than you could know
you have shown me more than you could show
you have given me more than you could give
you have filled this pain that was within

i always knew it could never be true
to be loved by you
i always knew i could never change
or rearrange the way i feel
this world stops and stares,
but it's not aware of my love for you

you have comforted me more than you could know
you have shown me more than you could show
you have given me more than you could give
you have filled this pain that was within

i always look and observe that
you're so much more than i deserve
i always look and fear the day
you'll leave and won't be near
there's a world of things i always fear,
but most is that you might not care

you're all i need, you're all my heart desires
you gave me love, you opened up my eyes
you saved me from the darkness of the night
i love you more than i love life

good morning dear heaven (1998)

as i lie next to you,
my head against your chest,
i feel the warmth of your body.
i hear your heart through your breast.

i curl up next to you,
feeling safe in your arms.
there's nothing for me to worry about,
for you protect me.

your eyes fall shut
and you go sound asleep.
i wonder… can you feel me?
i wonder what you dream.

i watch you, every move you make.
i would be content forever like this,
living off the sound of you breathing
and the steady hum of traffic outside.

when the sun comes up
and you start to wake,
i hush you back to sleep
and pull the window shade.

i cover your face from the light
and i muffle sounds from the street
cause i know you sleep better that way.
this is what heaven should be.

in love with you (1998)

as i sit and listen to
    the still,
        the steady,
            the cold,
i often wonder at you
    and where,
        and how,
            and what.

these days my mind is never blank.
    always racing,
      chasing,
           and up against time's back.
i should learn to stop and thank
    you a little more,
        a little for
            all those times you saved me.

do you think i depend on you too much
    for life,
        for love,
            for warmth?
or am i just addicted to your touch,
    no less,
        no little,
            no more?

together we become one (1998)

san francisco on the horizon
as i watch the waves roll by.
you sit on the rocks,
lovely and carefree this autumn day.

we speak not much
for thoughts transcend words.
our love fills the sky
and the clouds float away.

i cling to you like no other
and we grow together.
we become one,
floating down life's river.

but as the stream nears the sea
i hear your lowly voice.
sunrise illuminates the horizon
and looks upon us with approval.

we have learned to know what love is.

not long enough (1998)

there's a certain way i feel about you,
and words can't say what it means
'cause when they do it's not always true.
all i know is i love you
and you love me. i know it's real
'cause i can feel it inside you and inside me.

i could hold you forever
and it wouldn't be long enough.
we would gaze at the stars
until the sun came up.
and as the sunrise stared in our eyes
i'd say "i love you."
i don't think there's anything
i wouldn't do for you.

there's this certain look in your eyes,
i call it love. no mask could ever hide so much
and i trust it will always be this way.
it will always stay the same.
i've locked you to my heart
and thrown away the key.

animal crackers (1998)

i'd give anything to hold you next to me.
i wouldn't care what else we did.
i would be content to sit in bed with you
and eat animal crackers.
i'll let you eat all the bears
if you let me eat all the monkeys.
the rest of them we can divvy up
because they're not the ones that really matter.
when the sun goes down
we have to save what's left for breakfast.
but just don't forget,
we haven't even had dessert for dinner yet.

bedroom (1998)

pull down the window shade
and turn out the lights.
all i want to think of
is you tonight.

iii. requiems

shattered (1997)

my world has been shattered
like glass dropped upon a cold stone floor.
a void. complete in its existence.
but this void will be filled.
i will regress to the company of one.
i will regress to the point of no return.

please don't leave me, don't forsake me now.
don't repeat what has been done.
just try to love me, find it in your heart somehow.

i could never give my love to anyone else.
the risk is too great, and i am not that strong.
as long i have you to hold me up, be my support,
i will get by with nothing but a broken heart.

even though i can't have the whole of you,
i give you the whole of me.
understand you're all i have
and you're all i'll ever be.

promise me you will never leave.
don't shatter it all, for you are all i have left.

broken up low down dirty heart (1998)

since i've got this hole in my heart
i guess i'll be learning to play the part
a little bit better
and a little bit longer
than i had ever anticipated.

do you think i'll get paid any overtime at all,
or will i just be forced to leave and crawl
out the office door
on the dirty floor
into the streets of this city?

maybe i should call a cab so it seems,
or maybe a car service or limousine.
that would be nice,
but i'd have to pay the price.
and i'm just too fucking cheap for that.

i'd rather walk home past all the slums
than spend my hard-earned money on a car or bus.
i'll just risk getting mugged
by some low-down thug.
in the end it'll be okay.

have you ever had to play the part
of a low down dirty cheap broken heart?
i don't recommend it
for it's not a friendly
way to learn to live.

dead skin cells (1998)

like old fingernail clippings
i drop to the floor
at your feet
looking up at you

curved and curled
i lie naked
detached
and somehow shameless

with dirt on my backside
i wait
with not a hope
of being washed

i'm scarred
with growth unchanging
thrown out to rot
and become the dirt

trampled upon
rejected and torn
misused
by your abuse

alone and cold
withered
and old
i meet the earth again

a lament (1999)

like an angel dead in my arms
i hear day approaching.
like fire burning in my eyes
i feel your beauty.

engulfed in these flames
i become overwhelmed
as i begin my descent
to the unknown below.

i sleep with open eyes
to guard and protect,
and like you in my arms,
guardian angel cold and wet.

like a witch burned at the stake
i fly heavenward
and i feel no pain
as i swim in the sky.

a cloud blocks my eyes
like your hair in my face,
i search for meaning
through the haze.

unknown and unyielding
as a rosebud in winter
i lie in your arms
to be an angel's dead man.

cayendo (1997)

anteayer te amé,
te amé con todo que tuvé.
ayer mi amor crezó,
te amé con más que tuvé.
hoy mi amor caíste.
goteando de nubes, cayendo de cielo.

the day before yesterday i loved you
i loved you with all i had.
yesterday my love grew,
i loved you with more than i had.
today my love fell.
dripping from the clouds, falling from the sky.

your antique angel (1998)

somewhere in a room i sit
biding my time,
waiting for you to come.
but alas, i know you won't.
the thought that you might is nice.
i'll at least enjoy that for a while.

this morning you might have stepped out,
heading this way to come and see me.
your every intent was to show me you cared.
but before long you were sidetracked.
you'd follow alleyways and backstreets,
going off with a stranger or two.
and maybe, just maybe, if you're lucky
one might invite you to his house.
and we know what that would bring.
probably a night of fun, that goes without saying.
that's when i forget my hopes
of ever seeing you here again.

don't take notice that you've forgotten me.
i'm gone now, left here to die away,
just like all people do one day.
i guess i'm just being punished
for all those mean things i did and said.
i just wish that one last time you'd see me,
and we could spend one last night in bed.

i still remember your touch.
i can feel it like is was yesterday.
i still remember your breath.
i feel it on my back again.
but sometimes even memories are too late,
and dreams are better off forgotten.
maybe if we never dreamed in the first place
we wouldn't have to worry about getting hurt,
or hurting somebody else.

i know it's not easy for you to do this.
it's too much pain to even look at my face.
it brings back all those memories
of how we used to be when i was young.
i'm as light and brittle as an autumn leaf now,
and i don't blame you for not wanting to touch me.
just forget i ever even asked to see you
as you go on your merry way.

one day you'll grow old,
you'll be stuck in a room just like this.
your feet will be cold
and the blanket just never seems to stretch far
    enough
and nobody else is there to pull it.
that's when you'll realize how alone you are,
and how much you wish you still had me.
but don't worry, i'll be there by your side.
angels never forget true love.

parting is such sweet sorrow (1995)

the day's gone by
and the sun's gone down.
i don't know what to do anymore about you.
i'm living this life upside down.
don't wanna cry cause i'm cryin' for you.
don't know what to do cause i'm lost without you.

the sun comes up
and the nights all gone.
i'm scared, i'm tired, i'm here all alone.
i wish you were not gone.
my sorrow is sweet and i'm down on the floor.
i'm stoned on you man and i need a lot more.

the day's at an end,
my life is at rest.
i know you'll return
and my life will be at its best.
i'm looking for you, come on in a few.
together, forever? if only i knew.

parting is such sweet sorrow:
you say good-bye and slam the door.
parting is such sweet sorrow:
i don't wanna say good-bye anymore.
parting is such sweet sorrow:
it's something i can't bear to do.
parting is such sweet sorrow: with you.

distance (1998)

the sky becomes dark,
the horizon being inconsistent tonight.
so, too, my thoughts become inconsistent
as my mind sinks to a place deep within.

i focus on you. i focus on love.
then i focus on nothing at all.
grace overwhelms the dancers in my head.
it is art which i have a passion for.

art comes from the soul, a deep expression,
fulfilling voids you've known since you left the womb.
indeed, we all have left the womb,
for absence from Her womb is to be human.

yet, there is a time we visit that place again.
we become as a child, crawling, skipping,
chasing butterflies in the wind,
only to find we have melted back into the Goddess.

lucifer (1997)

the dew drips
    from a rose petal

onto a single sliver
    of razor blade grass

an angel falls down
    from the heavens

on a landslide
    into the depths

strident utterances of the night (1997)

i step into the dark and blackened night,
feeling the dampened sting of the cold breeze
as the space between my toes screams at me.
the air's filled with heart-trembling fright.
a basket full of wool socks could not warm
any foot or mittens for hand or face.
i gaze across the fields, where moonbeams grace
each strand of grass an unsheathed blade forlorn.
distance lurks, breeze blowing a dog's yawp here.
chill of death, murky depths depart silent
to a world below in eternity.
falling star fire hazard, the old sword falls.
new battles, new loves, new deaths to lament
and even hold pure. thy soul shall be free!

woe is my heart (1997)

heaven sweet hell,
    teach me thy ways
put on my lips the words
    of your speaking
show me the path
    to your love abiding
hold in your arms my own self
    of wretchedness
whisper your knowing
    into my ear
place your sweet tongue
    inside my mouth
scorn my wrongdoing and correct me
    to righteousness
lead me the way
    in thy grace everlasting

a commendation (1999)

in your bosom i lie abreast,
discomforted by my
inability to speak clearly.

unutterable thoughts become clear
as i am commended to you,
your body, your spirit.

my focus is unchanging,
for i know where i am going
and from where i came.

the intensity of solitude
has proven itself worthy
of sacred and spiritual devotion.

and with graceful magnitude
i worship love as i overturn
my soul to a Greater Power.

with my head in your lap
but my thoughts in the sky
i look down to you.

i greet the sun and the moon,
and all other elements of creation
as i leave this world behind.

from earth's womb i was thrust
and into the earth my body shall return,
but my spirit will rest elsewhere.

and until the last petal of the daisy falls
and the fire turns up nothing but ashes,
remember me as your only true love.

alone, without you (1997)

i go to that place
unadorned, true.
my thoughts are completely
focused on you.
i hold in my hand
a certain kind of pleasure.
i miss you, my love,
i cry without measure.

other early poems

i. associations

opera (1998)

suns rise at dawn
and clouds
cover skies

days die at night
and moons rise
in silence

mathematics (1996)

careful thoughts
on devout matters
never leave
jumbled thoughts
untangled inside ones
global sphere
around the nucleus
that controls feelings of
euphoria

you never know a child (1999)

i look back and see
how you never listened
to my pleas
that i knew who i was

you insisted you knew better
that i would change
time would tell
but you've locked me in

do you know what it means
to be kept captive?
my face is caked
with blood and dirt

you never know a child
or who they really are
until you tie them up
implicate them in your sin

don't extend your hand
for i've seen the truth
and would rather have nothing
than be part of your lie

for i have no secrets here

existence (1997)

can i love you in this way
or would it be wrong?
please don't push me away

my love for you is too strong
for my own good
and i cannot control this

how do you love me?
(or do you love me at all?)
are you a friend or an enemy?

do you speak honestly
or are you filled with lies?
blood drips from your tongue

unbecoming of your station
and makes it hard to tell
what those red letters really mean

but if you had your way
my mere existence
the very thought of my kind

would be an abomination

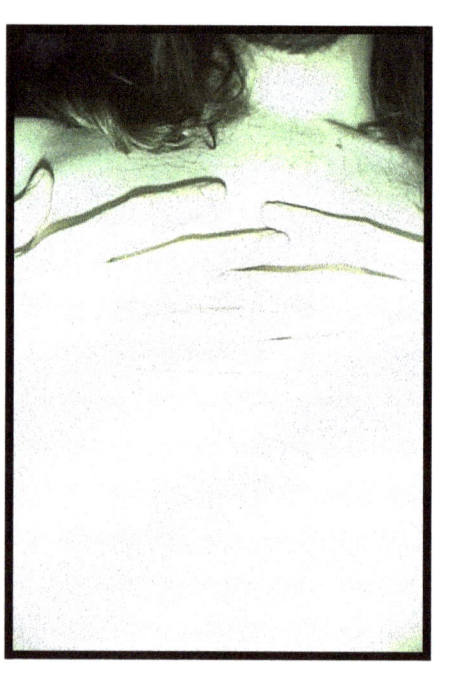

you ever loved me (1998)

i died of a cold broken heart
afraid of the dark, crying
unable to see

so did it matter if there was no light?

i loved you with all my heart
but then it was finished, leaving
unable to agree

so did it matter if you ever loved me?

set my mind up higher (1999)

i don't want you
never want you
don't need you
don't believe you

to believe myself
is hard enough;
to accept me
for who i am.

i thought it was easy
but i forgot to forget,
now i remember
such sarcasm:

come home
and be healthy,
be what i want
you to be,

(a hypocritical christian
mother once said.)
think i'd rather lay in bed,
cry my heart out my head,

drown my eyes
in a stream of prayer,
salute to consciousness
in a realization of self.

set my mind up higher
and burn the brightest fire.

stone cast aside (1997)

unequally treated in an unequal world
what else can you expect?

let me be alone in this expanse
and release me from your grip
let me have one more chance
to break away from this

why do you shudder when a man sheds tears
bears his feelings, thoughts, and loves?

it takes a bigger man to admit his fears

i am a stone cast aside
because its luster is not as bright

and i am afraid
you will never see how i shine
all polished up

where do you stand? (1997)

words roll off your tongue
and find their way down

you have no anxiety to speak
yet you seem filled with fear

do you believe what you say
or do you regret such accusations?

have you been brainwashed, confused,
and see me for the sinner?

i wonder,
where do you stand?

shadowed (1997)

there is something
in the way

i'm tied to a chair
—blindfolded—

or maybe
your hands are cupped
over my eyes
like a game of "guess who!"
that never ends

either way
—somehow—
you crept up behind
and managed to take hold

you might as well
have gouged out my eyes
with burning red spears

i am helpless
on my own

you are a cataract

only a surgical process
can remove you
and i am afraid of needles

we are
—forever—
one

i am
—trapped—
in your

shadow

a battle cry (1999)

in an attempt to
come to terms with myself
i wrestle with your soul
fight for your approval

i've always based my reality
on your dreams
and never gave a second thought
to what i wanted

but now i realize
the importance of self-care
and if i don't please me
how can i ever please you?

i have visions and dreams
sometimes even nightmares
but i can never escape my fears
if i don't face them first

i am at war with myself
unable to balance two worlds
but i'll never lay down my life
unless it's in exchange for another

hear my battle cry

purgatory (1998)

to whom do you belong
and to what god do you pray?
(or do you pray at all?)

did i kick dirt in your eyes
asking thoughtless questions?
did i spread ashes a little too soon
after burning the dead?

if the world ended tonight
would you end up in heaven?
(or do you believe in heaven at all?)

thorn (1997)

pull me down
and force me into your sin
make me love your desire

take me away
from what i used to be
to become part of you

turn me around
push me down
crown me with golden crowns

push thorns into my skin
pierce my side
and punish me

tumble these things
on top of me
bundled to my heart

wait…
do i want to make
this exchange

or not?

crisp leaves (1996)

autumn
everything's dead, gone
or moving away

crisp leaves fall
to the ground

to the floor

to what god
do you pray?

sail away
on an abandoned ship
—go far—

escape this death
and smothering love

dark waters—rage—

is your god
from above?

and what lies
—fathoms—
below?

ii. absolutions

a daisy, a fire (1999)

a daisy is more than a flower,
a fire is more than a flame
and a burning daisy is more
than a perishing plant: it's a shining soul

titanic (1998)

life lived without love
is like erecting
the world's largest ship
and never setting sail

dark rain (1999)

love falls relentlessly like rain
dripping in a shower
every moment, every hour
and each night i drown
drenched in your body

come celebrate with me (1999)

come celebrate with me, my love,
so we can sing against the blue sky
and i can praise you and your body
for the work of art it is.

to touch you is like heaven
and to hold you is like paradise.
at the very thought of your body
i am consumed by rapture
and my heart drowns in happiness
for it is you that i love.

wide-eyed amazement (1999)

and i stand in wide-eyed amazement
at your body, and also your grace,
even in rage it all shines right through
and i am no less addicted to you.

we hold back secrets from the world,
not from each other, but kept to ourselves.
i write you, praising your beauty,
i give you my all, 'tis my duty.

love and art (1999)

as a viscous cycle of words
races forth vehemently,
your slender figure calms me

as you glide across the floor.
Picasso waltzes nearby,
perhaps a faint Miró;

as if you descended from their brush.
such an exotic complexion,
you are breathtaking

yet we are locked behind
those boundaries: artist and viewer.
but such consent could no sooner

rise to meet us;
i come to greet you
and we break all the rules.

but what could they do,
even in that gallery
before Dalí and Degas,

we consummate our love
and compensate for our loss.
but before long we must part

for i am love, you are art.
we meet in the middle, unfixed,
for love can only know

what art insists.

love like a vampire (1999)

i rise to heaven
with a graceful sway
like a fairy dancing
across still waters

i am filled with anticipation
a divine poet of night song
painter of words who
through darkness shines bright

i lay down in the ashes
of dead vampires
ravaged and raveled bodies
conquered by daylight

desire is sparked
by these kindled daisies
my body soars
and i fly across the land

like a butterfly
i rest on your blossom
thirsty for nectar
as i sink my teeth in

your body vibrates
with passion
but is soon drained
of all energy

your eyes roll backward
and at the point of death
i give you a choice:
yet more or set free?

but of course
you begged
and now i give you
all that you need

you are mine
we are companions
you become accustomed
to my love like a vampire

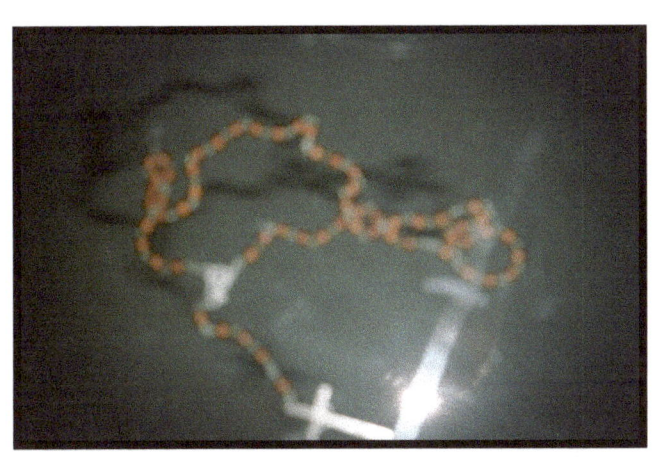

invincible flower (1999)

silence drowns my soul
like a wilted daisy
longing to be whole, stricken
and in pieces

i am trapped in a box
screaming and hopeless
barred behind locked doors
why won't you let me be?

you push me into fire
a dark, black death
cursed and filthy
condemned to hell

i am worn and numb
ravaged, splintered
in this isolation
but you keep me waiting

you are a devil
a threat to society
with your torture
and abuse

prayers are silent
voices crack in screams
i am isolated in this place
of dark nightmares

but within this sphere
i live full and free, alone
as i purge my fear
and become a burning daisy

on my own

absolution (1999)

i see your reflection in the rain
and am reminded of your beauty
while the quiet of this evening
only makes me miss you more

in my mind we are constantly together
chasing butterflies in the wind
through fields of daisies

at night we sleep by campfire
naked under blankets of sky
and in the morning we wake with sunrise

sometimes reality is too real
and i am alone, helpless without you
but at the moment we are reunited
all sins of separation will be absolved

faith (1999)

faith lacks the ability to know
the resolve to let go
to think and be clear
the ability to say, to hear
faith is to believe but not comprehend
faith is not fearing inevitable end

iii. dimensions

whore (1998)

love without trust
is like giving your house keys
to a complete stranger
and wondering
why you were robbed

my house, my love (1998)

sailboats cannot lure me there
and neither can the dawn
for nothing brings me out of this house
except your eyes

please do not question
my domestic existence
nor my blindness

this treason must remain
unspoken

to touch you is like heaven
hell is what separates us
with no god or saint to intervene

let my house be within these walls
with corners dark
and love unshaken—trapped—
behind closed doors

trapped within you (1996)

i feel your breath
across my chest
the touch of your lips

your body
—trapped—
inside my soul

while i am
—trapped—
within you

denied your love (1997)

turn off the lights
before you cross the room
amid this conflict

love is all
i seem to feel

i call to you
—silently—
but my breath
reveals my demise

you stare at me
from behind your eyes
truth bleeding
down your cheek

you ignore
my bliss

and though
it cannot be hidden
it will always be denied

rosebud (1996)

drop a lovely petal
upon this impure existence
we call life

is it a thing
of beauty?

or is it horror?

reality depth (1998)

life is a dream
and sleep a form of death

dreams are nothing
but thoughts
it is said

a dark well overflows
—are you drowning?—
gasping for breath

aimlessly lost
in nightmares

or—in reality—
the depths
of your

desire

late night past-times (1997)

all those nights you gazed
at the luminous heavens and its stars

all those nights you listened
to the drone of looming thunderstorms

all those nights you felt
the breeze coming in from the east

> i wonder, were they wasted moments
> or beautiful, intimate memories?

all those nights you stared
at the t.v., watching the late, late show

all those nights you read
the dark tales of Edgar Allan Poe

all those nights you listened
to the dreadful music of Nirvana

    i wonder, were they wasted moments
    or beautiful, intimate memories?

all those nights you looked
in my eyes and said "i love you"

all those nights you fondled
my chest and ran your hands through my hair

all those nights you jacked off
up there in your room

    i wonder, were they wasted moments
    or beautiful, intimate memories?

orgasm (1999)

being alone is a treasure
a tarnished soliloquy
to cherish every moment
as if it were the last

i can satisfy my urges
without worrying about someone
else rising to please them
and then not doing so

alone is the most
intimate way to be
because i know all
the buttons to push

the words to say
to make it feel that way
over
and over

again

river run dry (1997)

sometimes i am empty
completely void
like a river run dry
but yet i somehow
drown myself

for you to find me (1999)

it's quiet
and our walls
echo sound and light
in a catapult
racing outward

i scream
silenced by dreams
and the outside world
which waits
and hallucinates

i linger
silently tortured
and perturbed
lost and absurd
all alone

i break
unable to finish
my work
left incomplete
and unheard

for you to find me

distant land (1998)

somewhere in a distant land
i hope you hear me
and what it is i need

i'm out here alone
and don't know what to say
or sure as hell what to do

please send an emergency crew
communications are down
and satellites are spinning

wires are crossed and
infrastructure needs repair
so we can get in touch again

i'm out here screaming, fighting
to get back to you
lost in a distant land

can you hear my cry?

in dreams i shall forget (1999)

is this heaven
or hell?
i cannot discern
the difference

i try to forget the past
dwell not on mortality
nor of what i am
and how i became it

am i stuck in a maze
with no way out?
memory is painful
and life is like a dream

never remembering
completely the joy
never forgetting
fully the sadness

i miss you bittersweetly (1999)

i sit at night and reminisce
about all those memories
and how i miss
the thoughts and fragments
of your poetic words

oh, how i miss the way things were

there's no way i can do without you
yet time is a garden
and we have to let it grow
but even in this ever after
i still can't let you go

i miss you bittersweetly

rain cloud (1998)

where is your heart?
where have you flown to?
don't dare say to me
you're finished and you're through.

missing (1998)

i remember you
and think of you often
over tears

the pain of being
without you
is too much to bear

empty (1995)

i stand in a ring of fire
surrounded by silence
amid abounding ruefulness

—there are no words—
—no one is here—
—you are gone—

a scent of melancholy
fills the air
as i push against darkness
—incomplete—

treacherous burdens
press me flat
against the wall
feet dangling over spikes

what happens when i fall?

a flake of snow
lands on my brow
and soon another
—soft, gentle—

have i sensed your presence
or is this place
as empty as i feel?

black is brown
as everything fades
into corrupt dreams
—nightmares—
and i am surrounded
by the void
falling swiftly, falling down

into infinity

i'll find you in the rainbows (1998)

don't say goodbye
for i am with you still
as a speck of dust
or grass upon fields
somewhere in the universe
or across glassy seas
our spirits are connected
you are a part of me

iv. conclusions

flight (1999)

angel fell
from the sky

falling high
fall to die

and we all
wonder why

and how it is
an angel dies

i am not here (1999)

i am not here.
i'm not real.
no. do you see me?
your hand in mine?
no earth, no loss, no time.
i am a hologram,
an earthbound
piece of lonely happiness.
you a virgin from heaven,
a careless dyke for christ;
sweet angel lost your wings.
evangelical sings
sings sings sings,
and you ask me
one more time,
"did you ever find jesus?"
i replied:
"no, i never knew i lost him."

live me well (i'll give you that) (1999)

my eyes are sometimes blind
to the face of your happiness:
i can be such a selfishrottenchild.

but when i see your smile
i know what love is: freedom;
and i must let you carve your path.

they said it'd never last—
yet did we prove them wrong?
no need to prove what's known.

living well is the best revenge, you said.
and you have lived me well (i'll give you that).

burden as i sing (1999)

life is a song
and sometimes a burden
as i sing
but yet i sing on

i bring food to the table
when i'm too anxious to eat
and tend to my garden
for harvest is coming

i burn bright
to light the path ahead
from midnight to dawn
my soul's secret lover

i do not fall prey to hate
or conformity
and through this i kindle
a dark fire

but life is a song
and sometimes a burden
as i sing
but yet i sing on

as though living in a dream

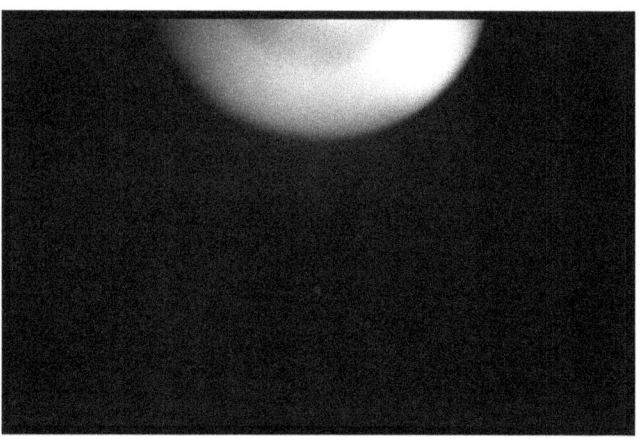

convergence (1999)

with a loss of words,
loss of thoughts,
pressed against my mind,
budding lips with agitation,
such a lonesome invitation
to discourse, discord and love
black… dark…
black darkness, hardness
pressed against hardness,
such largeness.
and with a loss of words,
loss of thoughts
and lips converge,
budding against my back,
the darkness, the cold black.

an elegy (1999)

i crawl across the ground
trying to reach you
clenching my teeth

the heavens beat down
my petals become weak
fall where angels trod

leaves catch fire
flowers burn fulgurously
i become a lightning rod

light bounces reflecting madly
skies grow deeply dark
i, a devoted rampart

slowly my fortress is vanquished
and i am overturned
in a relentless battle

consumed within an inferno
where freedom chokes
in gasps of air

i am not long for this world
but even in death
a burning daisy

never allays

the adage of old age (1999)

growing older yet wise
isn't really the truth.
wisdom is a concept,
the folly of youth

the older i grow
the clearer i see
that what i am
is all i need

humans glorify birth
and look down upon death
but i've come to think
old age is the best

i look forward in years,
and backward in days
all the while learning
to cherish old age

if i've learned anything
through all the years
it's that i know nothing
nor do i care

through the days of youth
we think we know it all
and worry about growing old
like a worn-out doll

but that wasn't really it.
we were afraid of something else.
we were afraid
of being our self

let age reveal its secret
and time be all well.
let me always be me,
not anyone else

mountaintop discourse (1999)

compassion sometimes has no recourse
to provide for that which it loves
and when life fleeting is not among us
so shall it rest on a mountaintop.

and there the mythic pixies play,
the fairies fly for freedom's sake
and all the while these sacred souls
find a cloud and heavenward float.

and it must be such a paradise
in those last, odd moments upon this earth.
it must be heaven in disguise
in that fleeting moment of discourse.

i rest within the shadows (1999)

i rest within the shadows
of the new fallen night
a luminous mourning
dressed in candlelight

dressed in the song
of an angel's prayer
on my knees
through the sky, to the air

i rest within the shadows
the sun behind by back
guarded by my love
for the darkness, the black

burning daisies (1999)

i'd rather burn
the brightest daisy
and reduce to ashes
than be a frozen rose
for eternity
bound to conformity

a chant (1999)

flames
ashes
smoke
choke
die
die
burn
churn
ashes
smoke
die
rise

about the artist

luke kurtis is an interdisciplinary artist focusing on the intersection of visuals, text, and tech. Ideas are the root of his work, forgoing any signature style in favor of conceptually-driven aesthetics and design. Select books include *Angkor Wat* and *exam(i)nation*, both part of an ongoing series that combines photography, writing, and design. His albums of experimental music include *obscure mechanics* and *electronic quartets*. He also makes short films, including *the woods are watching* and *convergence*, both documenting his installation art projects of the same names. His studio, bd-studios.com, publishes work both by himself and other artists and writers, and he is the co-founder of New Lit Salon Press. He lives and works in New York City's Greenwich Village.

Photo by Andrew P. Jones, Indian Beach, NC, July 1999

Also published by bd-studios.com

Poetry Books

Georgia Dusk by Dudgrick Bevins & luke kurtis
Route 4, Box 358 by Dudgrick Bevins
Train to Providence by William Doreski & Rodger Kingston
Angkor Wat by luke kurtis
exam(i)nation by luke kurtis
the immeasurable fold by luke kurtis
(This Is Not A) Mixtape for the End of the World
　　　by Daniel M. Shapiro

Artists' Books

The Animal Book by Michael Harren
Tentative Armor by Michael Harren
Here Nor There by Sam Rosenthal
Just One More by Jonathan David Smyth
Architecture and Mortality by Donald Tarantino
The Male Nude by Michael Tice
Retrospective by Michael Tice